To my son Luke, may Saint Abraam overshadow you with his guidance

COPYRIGHT © 2019
St Shenouda Press

All rights reserved. No part of this book may be reproduced in any manner without prior written permission from the publisher.

ST SHENOUDA PRESS
8419 Putty Rd,
Putty, NSW, 2330
Sydney, Australia

www.stshenoudapress.com

ISBN 13: 978-0-6485754-1-2

Since Saint Abraam was a little boy, he loved spending time in Church. Early Sunday mornings, he would wake up his parents to attend the Liturgy. Saint Abraam took any opportunity he could to pray and attend Sunday school. He loved being a deacon and helping in the altar.

Saint Abraam had a very kind and gentle heart. When he was a young boy, he would always notice the poor people on the street and would say a little prayer in his heart for them. He didn't notice the tall buildings around him or the exciting sights, he only noticed those who were poor.

As Saint Abraam grew older, his love and relationship with God became stronger. Soon after, with a lot of prayer and advice from his confession father, he decided to dedicate his life to God by becoming a monk. A monk is a person who lives in a monastery and gives all his time to God.

During his many years as a monk, he loved to work in silence and always helped those in need. Saint Abraam would do everything that he could to help around the monastery. No job was too big or too small for him. The older monks often relied on him for help.

Everyone around Saint Abraam knew he was a righteous and generous monk. After many years of being a monk, he was ordained as a Bishop. A Bishop is a monk who is responsible for the other monks, priests and people of a certain area. Saint Abraam was now known as the Bishop of Fayum.

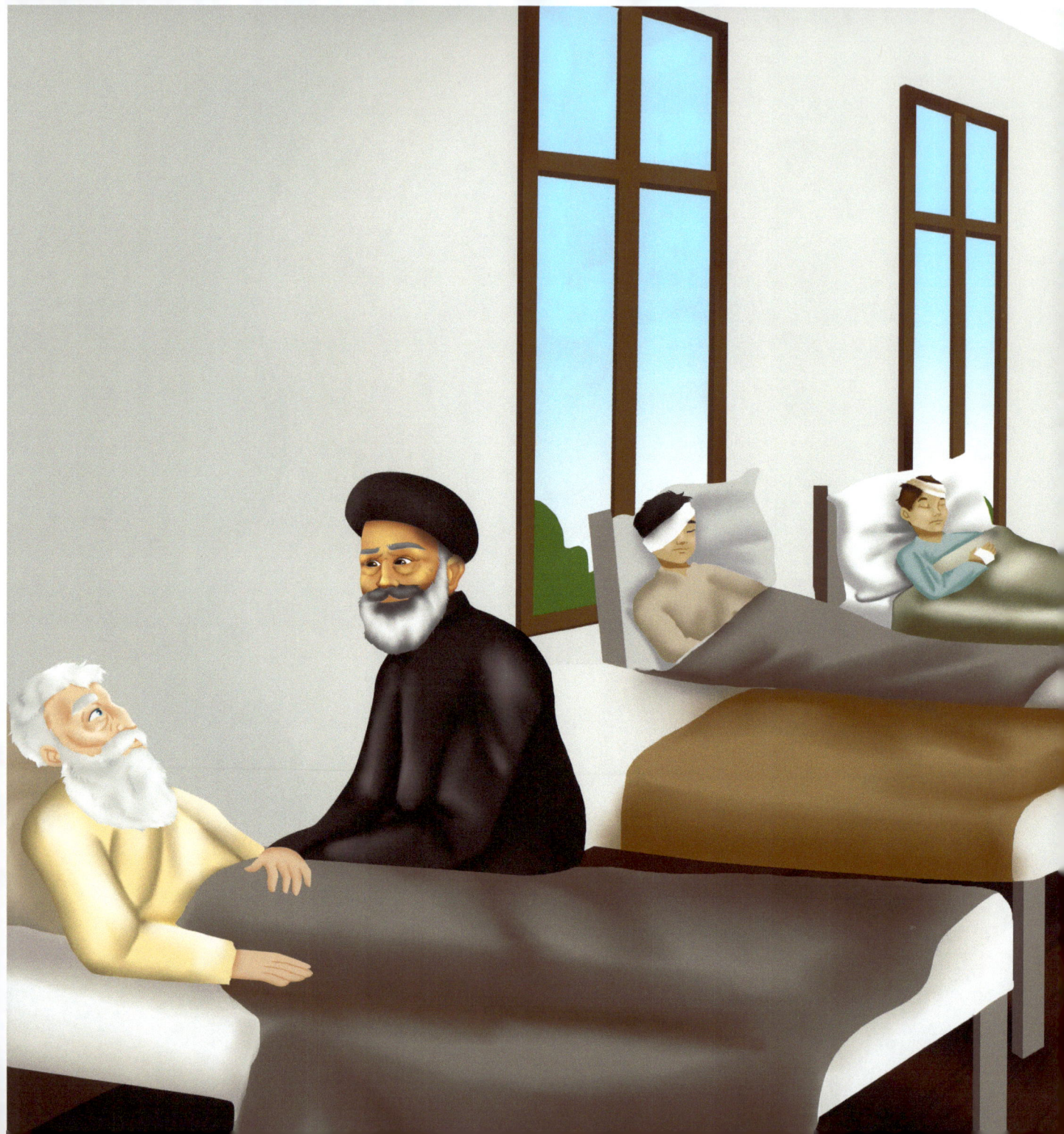

One day Saint Abraam felt in his heart he wanted to help others. He turned his home into a shelter for the homeless, orphaned and sick. He served and helped everyone there. People would bring those who were poor to his shelter as they knew they would be taken care of with love and mercy.

When people asked him for money, he would always give cheerfully. One day a lady came and asked him, "Could I have some money to feed my baby?" He replied, "I have no more money, take this scarf, sell it and use the money." The lady was very thankful even though she didn't know that this scarf was his only one, and that it kept him warm all winter!

Giving to the poor was something that made Saint Abraam feel so happy. He felt God's presence every time he gave to others. Saint Abraam would often leave baskets of clothes and food at people's doorsteps without them knowing. The Lord always blessed him.

Saint Abraam would spend a lot of time with people who were less fortunate. He would tell stories from the Bible and spread God's love. People who were sick were often brought to Saint Abraam and through his prayers, they were healed. God listened to Saint Abraam's prayers because he loved him so much!

After many years of joyful giving, Saint Abraam grew old. The people he had helped over time went to see him and prayed with him in his church. The love and care that was shown by Saint Abraam to those he served was now reflected in the growing faith of these people.

Saint Abraam always lived by the Bible verse that says, "God loves a cheerful giver" (2 Cor 9:7). In all that Saint Abraam did, in all that he gave, in all the ways he helped, he did so with a cheerful and generous heart. By his love and service towards those in need, many were able to witness Christ in him.

THE END

www.ingramcontent.com/pod-product-compliance
Lightning Source LLC
LaVergne TN
LVHW072117070426
835510LV00002B/90